PREDICTING
THE WEATHER

WEATHER WATCHERS... WEATHER WATCHERS... WEATHER WATCHERS... WEATHER WATCHER

MARI SCHUH

Rourke Educational Media
A Division of Carson Dellosa Education
rourkeeducationalmedia.com

ROURKE'S SCHOOL to HOME CONNECTIONS
BEFORE AND DURING READING ACTIVITIES

Before Reading: *Building Background Knowledge and Vocabulary*

Building background knowledge can help children process new information and build upon what they already know. Before reading a book, it is important to tap into what children already know about the topic. This will help them develop their vocabulary and increase their reading comprehension.

Questions and Activities to Build Background Knowledge:

1. Look at the front cover of the book and read the title. What do you think this book will be about?
2. What do you already know about this topic?
3. Take a book walk and skim the pages. Look at the table of contents, photographs, captions, and bold words. Did these text features give you any information or predictions about what you will read in this book?

Vocabulary: *Vocabulary Is Key to Reading Comprehension*

Use the following directions to prompt a conversation about each word.
- Read the vocabulary words.
- What comes to mind when you see each word?
- What do you think each word means?

Vocabulary Words:
- data
- meteorologists
- pressure
- radar

During Reading: *Reading for Meaning and Understanding*

To achieve deep comprehension of a book, children are encouraged to use close reading strategies. During reading, it is important to have children stop and make connections. These connections result in deeper analysis and understanding of a book.

Close Reading a Text

During reading, have children stop and talk about the following:
- Any confusing parts
- Any unknown words
- Text to text, text to self, text to world connections
- The main idea in each chapter or heading

Encourage children to use context clues to determine the meaning of any unknown words. These strategies will help children learn to analyze the text more thoroughly as they read.

When you are finished reading this book, turn to the last page for an **After Reading Activity**.

TABLE OF CONTENTS

Forecasting the Weather 4

Using Weather Tools 8

Changing Weather 20

Photo Glossary 22

Activity 23

Index 24

After Reading Activity 24

About the Author 24

FORECASTING THE WEATHER

Today is cloudy.

Could it rain soon?

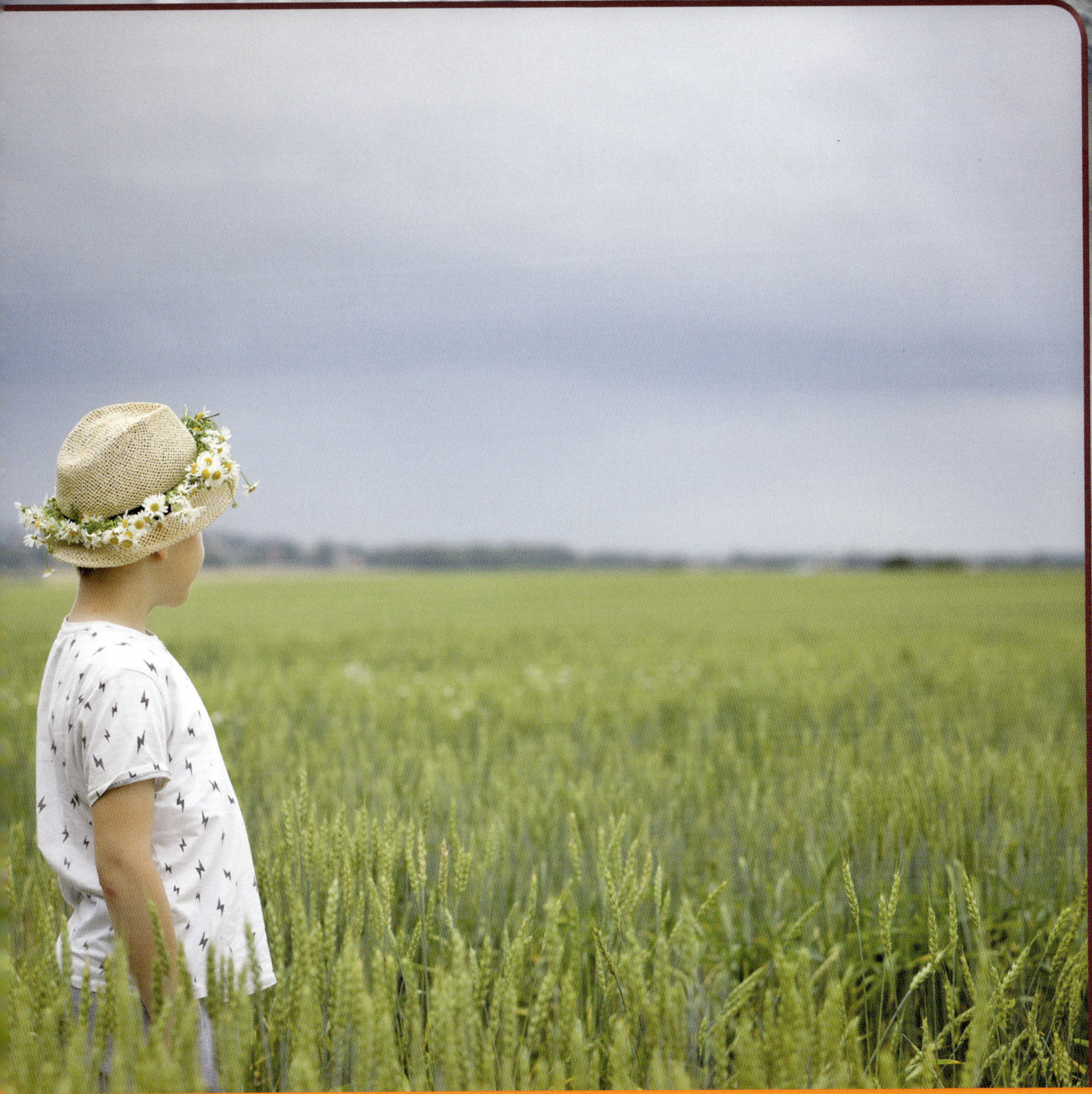

Meteorologists can tell us!

These scientists use tools to predict the weather.

Then, we can plan our day.

We can choose what to wear.

7

USING WEATHER TOOLS

Look at the weather balloon.

It carries tools.

It goes high in the sky.

All over the world, weather balloons are sent up in the air two times a day. They gather information.

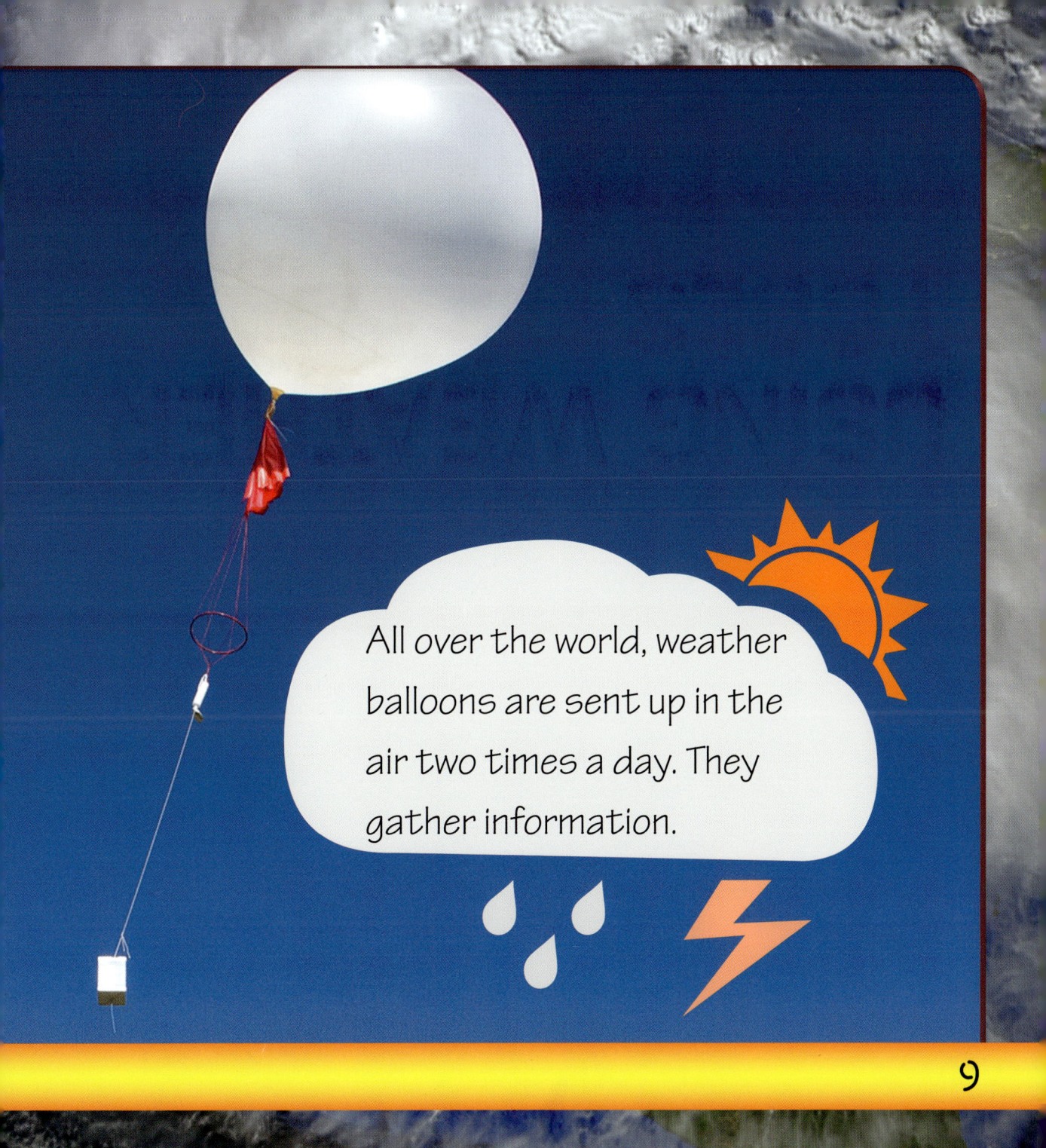

The tools measure wind and temperature.

They measure air **pressure** too.

11

A weather station gathers **data**.

It tells us about wind, rain, snow, and temperature.

13

Satellites watch Earth from space.

They take pictures of clouds and storms.

Satellites are very helpful for tracking dangerous hurricanes.

15

Radar shows us where storms are.

It also shows us how strong the storms are.

Red means lots of rain!

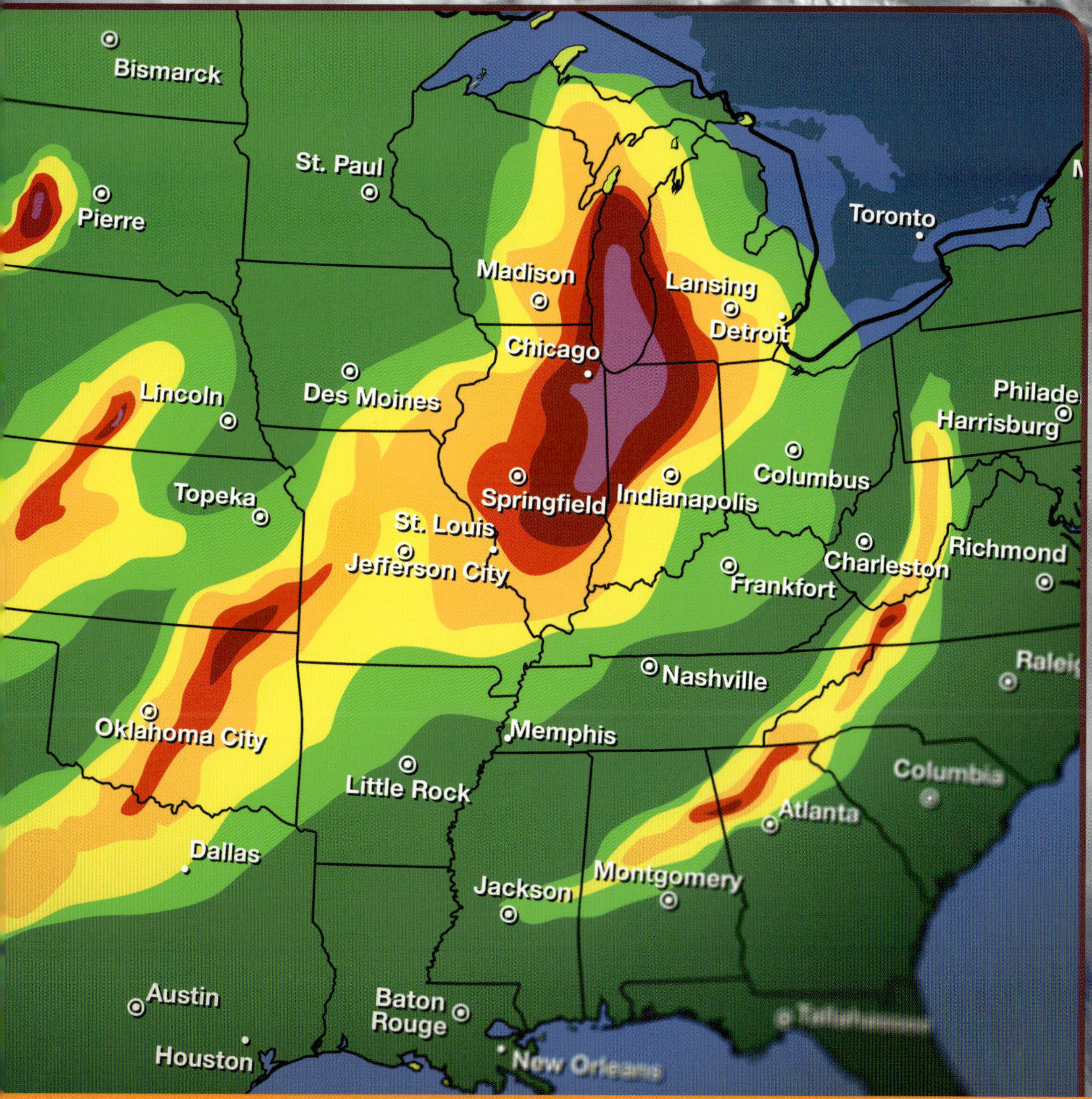
Bismarck
Pierre
St. Paul
Toronto
Madison
Lansing
Detroit
Chicago
Lincoln
Des Moines
Harrisburg
Columbus
Topeka
Springfield
Indianapolis
St. Louis
Jefferson City
Richmond
Charleston
Frankfort
Nashville
Oklahoma City
Memphis
Little Rock
Columbia
Atlanta
Dallas
Montgomery
Jackson
Austin
Baton Rouge
Houston
New Orleans

Computers help make weather forecasts.

We can see how hot or cold it may be.

Kyiv
16:22 EEST
Showers
19° 9°
15°
Forecast
17:00 18:00 19:00 20:00 21:00 22:00
18° 18° 17° 15° 14° 13°
Friday
Saturday 19° 9°
Sunday 22° 11°
Monday 25° 14°
Tuesday

CHANGING WEATHER

Weather always changes.

Many tools help us predict the weather. The forecast predicts it is a great day to play outside!

21

PHOTO GLOSSARY

data (DAY-tuh): Information that is collected and used to make decisions and predictions.

meteorologists (mee-tee-uh-RAH-luh-jists): Scientists who study Earth's atmosphere.

pressure (PRESH-ur): The force made by pressing on something.

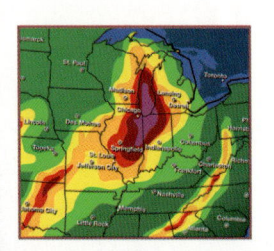

radar (RAY-dahr): A weather tool that sends out radio waves to find out where storms are, how strong they are, and how fast they are moving.

ACTIVITY: Pine Cone Weather Station

Pine cones can be simple weather tools. They can help you predict the weather!

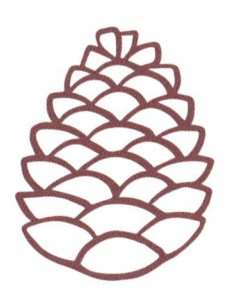

Supplies
four pine cones
tape or modeling clay
notebook
pen or pencil

Directions

1. Put four pine cones near one another in a safe place outside.
2. Use tape or modeling clay to keep the pine cones in their place.
3. Look closely at the pine cones in the morning. Are they open or closed? Write your answer in your notebook.
4. Pine cones open in dry weather. They close when rain is coming. Based on how your pine cones look, predict the weather for the day. Write your forecast in your notebook. At the end of the day, see if you were right!

ABOUT THE AUTHOR

Mari Schuh is the author of more than 300 nonfiction books for beginning readers, including many books about sports, animals, and stormy weather. She lives in Iowa with her husband and one very feisty house rabbit. You can learn more at her website: www.marischuh.com.

INDEX

computers 18
forecast(s) 18, 20
satellites 14

storms 14, 16
weather balloon(s) 8, 9
weather station 12

AFTER READING ACTIVITY

Watch a weather forecast on TV. Look closely. Watch how the meteorologists use radar and satellites in their forecasts. How do these tools help them predict the weather?

Library of Congress PCN Data

Predicting the Weather / Mari Schuh
(Weather Watchers)
ISBN 978-1-73162-842-8 (hard cover)(alk. paper)
ISBN 978-1-73162-837-4 (soft cover)
ISBN 978-1-73162-849-7 (e-Book)
ISBN 978-1-73163-329-3 (ePub)
Library of Congress Control Number: 2019909319

Rourke Educational Media
Printed in the United States of America,
North Mankato, Minnesota

© 2020 Rourke Educational Media

All rights reserved. No part of this book may be reproduced or utilized in any form or by any means, electronic or mechanical including photocopying, recording, or by any information storage and retrieval system without permission in writing from the publisher.

www.rourkeeducationalmedia.com

Edited by: Hailey Scragg
Cover design by: Kathy Walsh
Interior design by: Janine Fisher
Photo Credits: Cover ©Mike Mareen, ©mdesigner125; page 5: ©goodmoments; page 7: ©FrameStockFootages; page 9: ©Gwenvidig; page 11: ©Edward Haylan; page 13: ©TomekD76; page 15: ©aapsky; page 17: ©SpiffyJ; page 19: ©pressureUSA; page 21: ©FatCamera